THE HIDDEN WORDS OF
BAHA'U'LLAH

Translated by Shoghi Effendi

Illustrated by Corinne Randall

Intellect Bristol, UK, Chicago, USA

THE HIDDEN WORDS OF BAHA'U'LLAH

The Hidden Words is a collection of
meditational verse exploring the eternal
relationship between God and man.
Composed by the founder of the Bahá'i Faith
about the year 1858 as he walked, wrapt
in contemplation beside the River Tigris in
Baghdád, where He was exiled (1853-1863).

This illustrated version dives into
the essential moods and creative mysteries
of the word of God and rises to the surface of
this infinite ocean to leave a ripple of visual
illumination on the surface realm.

The Hidden Words

Part 1 *From the Arabic*

He is the Glory of Glories

This is that which hath descended

from the realm of glory, uttered

by the tongue of power and

might, and revealed unto the

Prophets of old.

We have taken the inner essence thereof and clothed it in the garment of brevity, as a token of grace unto the righteous, that they may stand faithful unto the Covenant of God, may fulfil in their lives His trust, and in the realm of spirit obtain the gem of Divine virtue.

1
O SON OF SPIRIT!

My first counsel is this:
Possess a pure, kindly and
radiant heart, that thine may
be a sovereignty ancient,
imperishable and everlasting.

O SON OF SPIRIT!

The best beloved of all things in My sight is Justice; turn not away therefrom if thou desirest Me, and neglect it not that I may confide in thee. By its aid thou shalt see with thine own eyes and not through the eyes of others, and shalt know of thine own knowledge and not through the knowledge of thy neighbour. Ponder this in thy heart how it behoveth thee to be. Verily justice is My gift to thee and the sign of My loving kindness. Set it then before thine eyes.

3
O SON OF MAN!

Veiled in My immemorial being and
in the ancient eternity of My essence,
I knew My love for thee: therefore
I created thee, have engraved on
thee Mine image and revealed
to thee My beauty.

4
O SON OF MAN!

I loved thy creation, hence I created
thee. Wherefore, do thou love Me,
that I may name thy name and fill thy soul
with the spirit of life.

5
O SON OF BEING!

Love Me, that I may love thee.
If thou lovest Me not,
My love can in no wise reach thee.
Know this, O servant.

6
O SON OF BEING!

Thy Paradise is My love;
thy heavenly home, reunion with Me.
Enter therein and tarry not.
This is that which hath been destined for
thee in Our kingdom above and
Our exalted dominion.

7
O SON OF MAN!

If thou lovest Me, turn away from thyself; and if thou seekest My pleasure, regard not thine own; that thou mayest die in Me and I may eternally live in thee.

8
O SON OF SPIRIT!

There is no peace for thee save by renouncing thyself and turning unto Me; for it behoveth thee to glory in My name, not thine own; to put thy trust in Me and not in thyself, since I desire to be loved alone and above all that is.

9
O SON OF BEING!

My love is My stronghold; he that entereth therein is safe and secure, and he that turneth away shall surely stray and perish.

10
O SON OF UTTERANCE!

Thou art My stronghold; enter therein that thou mayest abide in safety. My love is in thee, know it, that thou mayest find Me near unto thee.

11
O SON OF BEING!

Thou art My lamp and My light is in thee. Get thou from it thy radiance and seek none other than Me. For I have created thee rich and have bountifully shed My favour upon thee.

12
O SON OF BEING!

With the hands of power I made thee and with the fingers of strength I created thee; and within thee have I placed the essence of My light. Be thou content with it and seek naught else, for My work is perfect and My command is binding. Question it not, nor have a doubt thereof.

13
O SON OF SPIRIT!

I created thee rich, why dost thou bring thyself down to poverty? Noble I made thee, wherewith dost thou abase thyself? Out of the essence of knowledge I gave thee being, why seekest thou enlightenment from anyone beside Me? Out of the clay of love I molded thee, how dost thou busy thyself with another? Turn thy sight unto thyself, that thou mayest find Me standing within thee, mighty, powerful and self-subsisting.

14
O SON OF MAN!

Thou art My dominion and My dominion perisheth not, wherefore fearest thou thy perishing? Thou art My light and My light shall never be extinguished, why dost thou dread extinction? Thou art My glory and My glory fadeth not; thou art My robe and My robe shall never be outworn. Abide then in thy love for Me, that thou mayest find Me in the realm of glory.

O Son of Light! Forget all save Me and commune with My spirit. This is the essence of My command, therefore turn unto it. O Son of Light! Forget all save Me and commune with My spirit. This is the essence of My command, therefore turn unto it. O Son of Light! Forget all save Me and commune with My spirit. This is the essence of My command, therefore turn unto it. O Son of Light! Forget all save Me and commune with My spirit. This is the essence of My command, therefore turn unto it. O Son of Light! Forget all save Me and commune with My spirit. This is the essence of My command, therefore turn unto it. O Son of Light! Forget all save Me and commune with My spirit. This is the essence of My command, therefore turn unto it. O Son of Light! Forget all save Me and commune with My spirit. This is the essence of My command, therefore turn unto it. O Son of Light! Forget all save Me and commune with My spirit. This is the essence of My command, therefore turn unto it. O Son of Light! Forget all save Me and commune with My spirit. This is the essence of My command, therefore turn unto it. O Son of Light! Forget all save Me and commune with My spirit. This is the essence of My command, therefore turn unto it. O Son of Light! Forget all save Me and commune with My spirit.

15
O SON OF UTTERANCE!

Turn thy face unto Mine and
renounce all save Me; for My
sovereignty endureth and My dominion
perisheth not. If thou seekest another
than Me, yea, if thou searchest
the universe for evermore,
thy quest will be in vain.

16
O SON OF LIGHT!

Forget all save Me and commune with My
spirit. This is of the essence of My
command, therefore turn unto it.

17
O SON OF MAN!

Be thou content with Me and seek
no other helper. For none but Me
can ever suffice thee.

18
O SON OF SPIRIT!

Ask not of Me that which We desire not
for thee, then be content with what We
have ordained for thy sake, for this
is that which profiteth thee, if
therewith thou dost content thyself.

19
O SON OF THE WONDROUS VISION!

I have breathed within thee a breath of My own Spirit, that thou mayest be My lover. Why hast thou forsaken Me and sought a beloved other than Me?

20
O SON OF SPIRIT!

My claim on thee is great, it cannot be forgotten. My grace to thee is plenteous, it cannot be veiled. My love has made in thee its home, it cannot be concealed. My light is manifest to thee, it cannot be obscured.

21
O SON OF MAN!

Upon the tree of effulgent glory I have hung for thee the choicest fruits, wherefore hast thou turned away and contented thyself with that which is less good? Return then unto that which is better for thee in the realm on high.

22
O SON OF SPIRIT!

Noble I created thee,
yet thou hast abased thyself.
Rise then unto that
for which thou wast created.

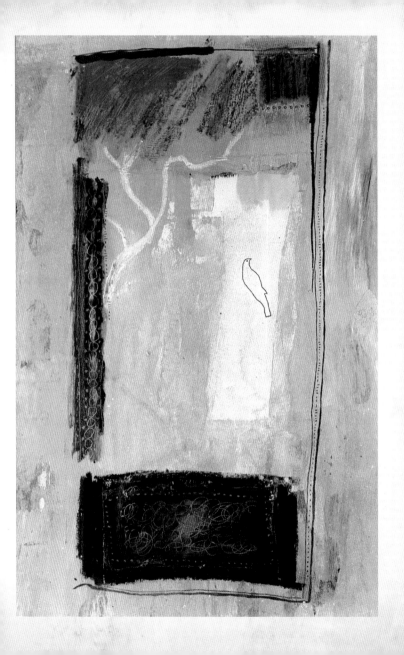

23
O SON OF THE SUPREME!

To the eternal I call thee, yet thou dost
seek that which perisheth.
What hath made thee turn away from
Our desire and seek thine own?

24
O SON OF MAN!

Transgress not thy limits, nor claim
that which beseemeth thee not. Prostrate
thyself before the countenance of thy God,
the Lord of might and power.

25
O SON OF SPIRIT!

Vaunt not thyself over the poor,
for I lead him on his way and
behold thee in thy evil plight and
confound thee for evermore.

26
O SON OF BEING!

How couldst thou forget thine own faults and busy thyself with the faults of others? Whoso doeth this is accursed of Me.

27
O SON OF MAN!

Breathe not the sins of others so long as thou art thyself a sinner. Shouldst thou transgress this command, accursed wouldst thou be, and to this I bear witness.

28
O SON OF SPIRIT!

Know thou of a truth: He that biddeth men be just and himself committeth iniquity is not of Me, even though he bear My name.

29
O SON OF BEING!

Ascribe not to any soul that which thou wouldst not have ascribed to thee, and say not that which thou doest not. This is My command unto thee, do thou observe it.

30
O SON OF MAN!

Deny not My servant should he ask anything from thee, for his face is My face; be then abashed before Me.

31
O SON OF BEING!

Bring thyself to account each day ere thou art summoned to a reckoning: for death, unheralded, shall come upon thee and thou shalt be called to give account for thy deeds.

32
O SON OF THE SUPREME!

I have made death a messenger of joy to thee. Wherefore dost thou grieve? I made the light to shed on thee its splendour. Why dost thou veil thyself therefrom?

33
O SON OF SPIRIT!

With the joyful tidings of light I hail thee: rejoice! To the court of holiness I summon thee; abide therein that thou mayest live in peace for evermore.

34
O SON OF MAN!

The spirit of holiness beareth unto thee the
joyful tidings of reunion; wherefore dost thou
grieve? The spirit of power confirmeth thee in
His cause; why dost thou veil thyself?
The light of His countenance doth lead thee;
how canst thou go astray?

35
O SON OF MAN!

Sorrow not save that thou art far from Us.
Rejoice not save that thou art drawing near
and returning unto Us.

36
O SON OF MAN!

Rejoice in the gladness of thine heart,
that thou mayest be worthy to meet Me and
to mirror forth My beauty.

37
O SON OF MAN!

Divest not thyself of My beauteous robe,
and forfeit not thy portion from My
wondrous fountain, lest thou shouldst
thirst for evermore.

38
O SON OF BEING!

Walk in My statutes for love of Me
and deny thyself that which thou desirest
if thou seekest My pleasure.

39
O SON OF MAN!

Neglect not My commandments if
thou lovest My beauty, and forget not
My counsels if thou wouldst attain
My good pleasure.

Wert thou to speed through the immensity
of space and traverse the expanse of heaven,
yet thou wouldst find no rest save in
submission to Our command and
humbleness before Our Face.

41
O SON OF MAN!

Magnify My cause that I may reveal
unto thee the mysteries of My greatness
and shine upon thee with the
light of eternity.

42
O SON OF MAN!

Humble thyself before Me,
that I may graciously visit thee.
Arise for the triumph of My cause,
that while yet on earth thou
mayest obtain the victory.

43
O SON OF BEING!

Make mention of Me on My
earth, that in My heaven I may
remember thee, thus shall Mine
eyes and thine be solaced.

44
O SON OF THE THRONE!

Thy hearing is My hearing, hear thou therewith. Thy sight is My sight, do thou see therewith, that in thine inmost soul thou mayest testify unto My exalted sanctity, and I within Myself may bear witness unto an exalted station for thee.

45
O SON OF BEING!

Seek a martyr's death in My path, content with My pleasure and thankful for that which I ordain, that thou mayest repose with Me beneath the canopy of majesty behind the tabernacle of glory.

46
O SON OF MAN!

Ponder and reflect. Is it thy wish to die upon thy bed, or to shed thy life-blood on the dust, a martyr in My path, and so become the manifestation of My command and the revealer of My light in the highest paradise? Judge thou aright, O servant!

47
O SON OF MAN!

By My beauty! To tinge thy hair with thy blood is greater in My sight than the creation of the universe and the light of both worlds. Strive then to attain this, O servant!

The sign of love is fortitude under My decree and decree and patience under My trials...

For everything
there is a...
sign.

48
O SON OF MAN!

For everything there is a sign.
The sign of love is fortitude under My
decree and patience under My trials.

49
O SON OF MAN!

The true lover yearneth for tribulation
even as doth the rebel for forgiveness
and the sinful for mercy.

50
O SON OF MAN!

If adversity befall thee not in My path,
how canst thou walk in the ways of them
that are content with My pleasure?
If trials afflict thee not in thy longing
to meet Me, how wilt thou attain
the light in thy love for My beauty?

51
O SON OF MAN!

My calamity is My providence, outwardly
it is fire and vengeance, but inwardly it is
light and mercy. Hasten thereunto that
thou mayest become an eternal light and
an immortal spirit. This is My command
unto thee, do thou observe it.

52
O SON OF MAN!

Should prosperity befall thee, rejoice not
and should abasement come upon thee,
grieve not, for both shall pass away
and be no more.

53
O SON OF BEING!

If poverty overtake thee, be not sad; for in
time the Lord of wealth shall visit thee.
Fear not abasement, for glory shall
one day rest on thee.

54
O SON OF BEING!

If thine heart be set upon this eternal,
imperishable dominion, and this ancient,
everlasting life, forsake this mortal
and fleeting sovereignty.

55
O SON OF BEING!

Busy not thyself with this world,
for with fire We test the gold
and with gold We test
Our servants.

56
O SON OF MAN!

Thou dost wish for gold and
I desire thy freedom from it.
Thou thinkest thyself rich in its
possession, and I recognize thy
wealth in thy sanctity therefrom.
By My life! This is My knowledge,
and that is thy fancy; how can
My way accord with thine?

57
O SON OF MAN!

Bestow My wealth upon My poor, that in heaven thou mayest draw from stores of unfading splendour and treasures of imperishable glory. But by My life! To offer up thy soul is a more glorious thing couldst thou but see with Mine eye.

58
O SON OF MAN!

The temple of being is My throne; cleanse it of all things, that there I may be established and there I may abide.

59
O SON OF BEING!

Thy heart is my home; sanctify it for My descent. Thy spirit is My place of revelation; cleanse it for My manifestation.

60
O SON OF MAN!

Put thy hand into My bosom, that I may arise above thee, radiant and resplendent.

61
O SON OF MAN!

Ascend unto My heaven, that thou mayest obtain the joy of reunion, and from the chalice of imperishable glory quaff the peerless wine.

62
O SON OF MAN!

Many a day hath passed over thee whilst thou hast busied thyself with thy fancies and idle imaginings. How long art thou to slumber on thy bed? Lift up thy head from slumber, for the Sun has risen to the zenith, haply it may shine upon thee with the light of beauty.

63
O SON OF MAN!

The light hath shone on thee from the
horizon of the sacred Mount and the spirit
of enlightenment hath breathed in the
Sinai of thy heart. Wherefore, free thyself
from the veils of idle fancies and enter
into My court, that thou mayest be fit for
everlasting life and worthy to meet Me.
Thus may death not come upon thee,
neither weariness nor trouble.

64
O SON OF MAN!

My eternity is My creation, I have
created it for thee. Make it the garment
of thy temple. My unity is My handiwork;
I have wrought it for thee; clothe thyself
therewith, that thou mayest be to
all eternity the revelation of
My everlasting being.

65
O SON OF MAN!

My majesty is My gift to thee, and My
grandeur the token of My mercy unto thee.
That which beseemeth Me none shall
understand, nor can any one recount.
Verily, I have preserved it in My hidden
storehouses and in the treasuries of
My command, as a sign of
My loving-kindness unto My servants
and My mercy unto My people.

66
O CHILDREN OF THE DIVINE
AND INVISIBLE ESSENCE!

Ye shall be hindered from loving Me and
souls shall be perturbed as they make
mention of Me. For minds cannot grasp
Me nor hearts contain Me.

67
O SON OF BEAUTY!

By My spirit and by My favour! By My mercy and by My beauty! All that I have revealed unto thee with the tongue of power, and have written for thee with the pen of might, hath been in accordance with thy capacity and understanding, not with My state and the melody of My voice.

68
O CHILDREN OF MEN!

Know ye not why We created you all from the same dust? That no one should exalt himself over the other. Ponder at all times in your hearts how ye were created. Since We have created you all from one same substance it is incumbent on you to be even as one soul, to walk with the same feet, eat with the same mouth and dwell in the same land, that from your inmost being, by your deeds and actions, the signs of oneness and the essence of detachment may be made manifest. Such is My counsel to you, O concourse of light! Heed ye this counsel that ye may obtain the fruit of holiness from the tree of wondrous glory.

69
O YE SONS OF SPIRIT!

Ye are My treasury, for in you I have
treasured the pearls of My mysteries
and the gems of My knowledge.
Guard them from the strangers amidst
My servants and from the
ungodly amongst My people.

70
O SON OF HIM THAT STOOD BY HIS OWN
ENTITY IN THE KINGDOM OF HIS SELF!

Know thou, that I have wafted unto thee
all the fragrances of holiness,
have fully revealed to thee My word,
have perfected through thee My bounty
and have desired for thee that
which I have desired for My Self.
Be then content with My pleasure
and thankful unto Me.

Write all that We have revealed unto thee with the ink of light upon the tablet of thy spirit. Should this not be in thy power, then make thine ink of the essence of thy heart. If this thou canst not do, then write with that crimson ink that hath been shed in My path. Sweeter indeed is this to Me than all else, that its light my endure for ever.

The Hidden Words

Part II *From the Persian*

In the Name of the Lord of Utterance,
the Mighty.

O YE PEOPLE THAT HAVE MINDS TO KNOW AND EARS TO HEAR!

The first call of the Beloved is
this: O mystic nightingale! Abide
not but in the rose-garden of
the spirit. O messenger of the
Solomon of love! Seek thou
no shelter except in the
Sheba of the well-beloved,
and O immortal phoenix!
dwell not save on the mount
of faithfulness. Therein is thy
habitation, if on the wings of
thy soul thou soarest to the
realm of the infinite and
seekest to attain thy goal.

2
O SON OF SPIRIT!

The bird seeketh its nest; the nightingale the charm of the rose; whilst those birds, the hearts of men, content with transient dust, have strayed far from their eternal nest, and with eyes turned towards the slough of heedlessness are bereft of the glory of the divine presence. Alas! How strange and pitiful; for a mere cupful, they have turned away from the billowing seas of the Most High, and remained far from the most effulgent horizon.

3
O FRIEND!

In the garden of thy heart plant
naught but the rose of love,
and from the nightingale of affection
and desire loosen not thy hold.
Treasure the companionship of the
righteous and eschew all
fellowship with the ungodly.

4
O SON OF JUSTICE!

Whither can a lover go but to the land
of his beloved? And what seeker findeth
rest away from his heart's desire?
To the true lover reunion is life, and
separation is death. His breast is void of
patience and his heart hath no peace.
A myriad lives he would forsake
to hasten to the abode of his beloved.

5
O SON OF DUST!

Verily I say unto thee: Of all men the most
negligent is he that disputeth idly and seeketh
to advance himself over his brother.
Say, O brethren! Let deeds, not words,
be your adorning.

6
O SON OF EARTH!

Know, verily, the heart wherein the least
remnant of envy yet lingers, shall never attain
My everlasting dominion, nor inhale the
sweet savours of holiness breathing from
My kingdom of sanctity.

7
O SON OF LOVE!

Thou art but one step away from the glorious
heights above and from the celestial tree of love.
Take thou one pace and with the next advance
into the immortal realm and enter the pavilion
of eternity. Give ear then to that which hath
been revealed by the pen of glory.

8
O SON OF GLORY!

Be swift in the path of holiness, and enter the heaven of communion with Me. Cleanse thy heart with the burnish of the spirit, and hasten to the court of the Most High.

9
O FLEETING SHADOW!

Pass beyond the baser stages of doubt and rise to the exalted heights of certainty. Open the eye of truth, that thou mayest behold the veilless Beauty and exclaim: Hallowed be the Lord, the most excellent of all creators!

10
O SON OF DESIRE!

Give ear unto this: Never shall mortal eye recognize the everlasting Beauty, nor the lifeless heart delight in aught but in the withered bloom. For like seeketh like, and taketh pleasure in the company of its kind.

11

O SON OF DUST!

Blind thine eyes, that thou mayest behold My beauty; stop thine ears, that thou mayest hearken unto the sweet melody of My voice; empty thyself of all learning, that thou mayest partake of My knowledge; and sanctify thyself from riches, that thou mayest obtain a lasting share from the ocean of My eternal wealth. Blind thine eyes, that is, to all save My beauty; stop thine ears to all save My word; empty thyself of all learning save the knowledge of Me; that with a clear vision, a pure heart and an attentive ear thou mayest enter the court of My holiness.

12
O MAN OF TWO VISIONS!

Close one eye and open the other.
Close one to the world and all that is
therein, and open the other to the
hallowed beauty of the Beloved.

13
O MY CHILDREN!

I fear lest, bereft of the melody of the
dove of heaven, ye will sink back to the
shades of utter loss, and, never having
gazed upon the beauty of the rose,
return to water and clay.

14
O FRIENDS!

Abandon not the everlasting beauty
for a beauty that must die,
and set not your affections
on this mortal world of dust.

15
O SON OF SPIRIT!

The time cometh, when the nightingale
of holiness will no longer unfold the inner
mysteries and ye will all be bereft
of the celestial melody and
the voice from on high.

of hidden mysteries of hidden mysteries of hidd
revealed in a single melody, revealed in a single
Myriads of mystic tongues, Myriads of mystic tong
ystic tongues Myriads of mystic tongues. Myriads of
of mystic find utterance in one speech; find utter
myriads in one and myriads and myriads and my
find and of hidden mysteries are of hidden mys
of hidden revealed in a single revealed in a single
revealed in a sing melody, melody, Myriads of mys
Myriads of mystic tongues. Myriads of mystic tong
find utterance in one speech; find utterance in
and myriads of hidden mysteries and myriads
are revealed in a single are revealed in a sin
single melody, single melody, single melody's
Myriads of mystic tongues, Myriads of mystic t
find utterance in one speech, find utterance in
of hidden mysteries of hidden mysteries of hidd
revealed in a single melody, revealed in a single
Myriads of mystic tongues, Myriads of mystic tong
ystic tongues Myriads of mystic tongues. Myriads of
of mystic find utterance in one speech; find utter
myriads in one and myriads and myriads and my
find and of hidden mysteries are of hidden mys
hidden revealed in a single revealed in a single

O ESSENCE OF NEGLIGENCE!

Myriads of mystic tongues find utterance
in one speech, and myriads of hidden
mysteries are revealed in a single melody;
yet, alas, there is no ear to hear,
nor heart to understand.

17
O COMRADES!

The gates that open on the Placeless stand
wide and the habitation of the loved one is
adorned with the lovers' blood, yet all but a
few remain bereft of this celestial city,
and even of these few, none but the smallest
handful hath been found with a pure
heart and sanctified spirit.

18
O YE DWELLERS IN THE HIGHEST PARADISE!

Proclaim unto the children of assurance that
within the realms of holiness, nigh unto the
celestial paradise, a new garden hath appeared,
round which circle the denizens of the realm
on high and the immortal dwellers of the
exalted paradise. Strive, then, that ye may
attain that station, that ye may unravel the
mysteries of love from its wind-flowers and
learn the secret of divine and consummate
wisdom from its eternal fruits. Solaced are the
eyes of them that enter and abide therein!

19
O MY FRIENDS!

Have ye forgotten that true and radiant morn,
when in those hallowed and blessed surroundings
ye were all gathered in My presence beneath the
shade of the tree of life, which is planted in the
all-glorious paradise? Awe-struck ye listened as
I gave utterance to these three most holy words:
O friends! Prefer not your own will to Mine, never
desire that which I have not desired for you,
and approach Me not with lifeless hearts,
defiled with worldly desires and cravings.
Would ye but sanctify your souls, ye would at
this present hour recall that place and those
surroundings, and the truth of My utterance
should be made evident unto all of you.

In the eighth of the most holy lines,
in the fifth Tablet of Paradise, He saith:

20
O YE THAT ARE LYING AS DEAD ON THE COUCH OF HEEDLESSNESS!

Ages have passed and your precious lives are well-nigh ended, yet not a single breath of purity hath reached Our court of holiness from you. Though immersed in the ocean of misbelief, yet with your lips ye profess the one true faith of God. Him whom I abhor ye have loved, and of My foe ye have made a friend. Notwithstanding, ye walk on My earth complacent and self-satisfied, heedless that My earth is weary of you and everything within it shunneth you. Were ye but to open your eyes, ye would, in truth, prefer a myriad griefs unto this joy, and would count death itself better than this life.

21
O MOVING FORM OF DUST!

I desire communion with thee, but thou wouldst put no trust in Me. The sword of thy rebellion hath felled the tree of thy hope. At all times I am near unto thee, but thou art ever far from Me. Imperishable glory I have chosen for thee, yet boundless shame thou hast chosen for thyself. While there is yet time, return, and lose not thy chance.

O SON OF DESIRE!

The learned and the wise have for long years
striven and failed to attain the presence of the
All-Glorious; they have spent their lives in search
of Him, yet did not behold the beauty of His
countenance. Thou without the least effort didst
attain thy goal, and without search hast obtained
the object of thy quest. Yet, notwithstanding,
thou didst remain so wrapt in the veil of self, that
thine eyes beheld not the beauty of the Beloved,
nor did thy hand touch the hem of His robe.
Ye that have eyes behold and wonder.

23
O DWELLERS IN THE CITY OF LOVE!

Mortal blasts have beset the everlasting candle,
and the beauty of the celestial Youth is veiled in
the darkness of dust. The chief of the monarchs
of love is wronged by the people of tyranny and
the dove of holiness lies prisoned in the talons
of owls. The dwellers in the pavilion of glory
and the celestial concourse bewail and lament,
while ye repose in the realm of negligence,
and esteem yourselves as of the true friends.
How vain are your imaginings!

24
O YE THAT ARE FOOLISH,
YET HAVE A NAME TO BE WISE!

———————

Wherefore do ye wear the guise of shepherds, when inwardly ye have become wolves, intent upon My flock? Ye are even as the star, which riseth ere the dawn, and which, though it seem radiant and luminous, leadeth the wayfarers of My city astray into the paths of perdition.

25
O YE SEEMING FAIR YET INWARDLY FOUL!

———————

Ye are like clear but bitter water, which to outward seeming is crystal pure but of which, when tested by the divine Assayer, not a drop is accepted. Yea, the sunbeam falls alike upon the dust and the mirror, yet differ they in reflection even as doth the star from the earth: nay, immeasurable is the difference!

26
O MY FRIEND IN WORD!

———————

Ponder awhile. Hast thou ever heard that friend and foe should abide in one heart? Cast out then the stranger, that the Friend may enter His home.

27
O SON OF DUST!

All that is in heaven and earth I have ordained
for thee, except the human heart, which I have
made the habitation of My beauty and glory;
yet thou didst give My home and dwelling to
another than Me; and whenever the
manifestation of My holiness sought His own
abode, a stranger found He there, and,
homeless, hastened unto the sanctuary of the
Beloved. Notwithstanding I have concealed
thy secret and desire not thy shame.

28
O ESSENCE OF DESIRE!

At many a dawn have I turned from the
realms of the Placeless unto thine abode,
and found thee on the bed of ease busied
with others than Myself. Thereupon, even
as the flash of the spirit, I returned to the
realms of celestial glory and breathed
it not in My retreats above unto
the hosts of holiness.

29

O SON OF BOUNTY!

Out of the wastes of nothingness, with the clay of My command I made thee to appear, and have ordained for thy training every atom in existence and the essence of all created things. Thus, ere thou didst issue from thy mother's womb, I destined for thee two founts of gleaming milk, eyes to watch over thee, and hearts to love thee. Out of My loving-kindness, 'neath the shade of My mercy I nurtured thee, and guarded thee by the essence of My grace and favour. And My purpose in all this was that thou mightest attain My everlasting dominion and become worthy of My invisible bestowals. And yet heedless thou didst remain, and when fully grown, thou didst neglect all My bounties and occupied thyself with thine idle imaginings, in such wise that thou didst become wholly forgetful, and, turning away from the portals of the Friend, didst abide within the courts of My enemy.

30
O BOND SLAVE OF THE WORLD!

Many a dawn hath the breeze of My
loving-kindness wafted over thee and found thee
upon the bed of heedlessness fast asleep.
Bewailing then thy plight it returned
whence it came.

31
O SON OF EARTH!

Wouldst thou have Me, seek none other than Me;
and wouldst thou gaze upon My beauty,
close thine eyes to the world and all that is
therein; for My will and the will of another
than Me, even as fire and water,
cannot dwell together in one heart.

32
O BEFRIENDED STRANGER!

The candle of thine heart is lighted by the hand
of My power, quench it not with the contrary
winds of self and passion. The healer of all
thine ills is remembrance of Me, forget it not.
Make My love thy treasure and cherish it
even as thy very sight and life.

33
O MY BROTHER!

Hearken to the delightsome words of My honeyed tongue, and quaff the stream of mystic holiness from My sugar-shedding lips. Sow the seeds of My divine wisdom in the pure soil of thy heart, and water them with the water of certitude, that the hyacinths of My knowledge and wisdom may spring up fresh and green in the sacred city of thy heart.

34
O DWELLERS OF MY PARADISE!

With the hands of loving-kindness I have planted in the holy garden of paradise the young tree of your love and friendship, and have watered it with the goodly showers of My tender grace; now that the hour of its fruiting is come, strive that it may be protected, and be not consumed with the flame of desire and passion.

35
O MY FRIENDS!

Quench ye the lamp of error, and kindle within your hearts the everlasting torch of divine guidance. For ere long the assayers of mankind shall, in the holy presence of the Adored, accept naught but purest virtue and deeds of stainless holiness.

36
O SON OF DUST!

The wise are they that speak not unless they obtain a hearing, even as the cup-bearer, who proffereth not his cup till he findeth a seeker, and the lover who crieth not out from the depths of his heart until he gazeth upon the beauty of his beloved. Wherefore sow the seeds of wisdom and knowledge in the pure soil of the heart, and keep them hidden, till the hyacinths of divine wisdom spring from the heart and not from mire and clay.

In the first line of the Tablet it is recorded and written, and within the sanctuary of the tabernacle of God is hidden:

37
O MY SERVANT!

Abandon not for that which perisheth an everlasting dominion, and cast not away celestial sovereignty for a worldly desire. This is the river of everlasting life that hath flowed from the well-spring of the pen of the merciful; well is it with them that drink!

38
O SON OF SPRIT!

Burst thy cage asunder, and even as the
phoenix of love soar into the firmament of
holiness. Renounce thyself and, filled with
the spirit of mercy, abide in the realm
of celestial sanctity.

39
O OFFSPRING OF DUST!

Be not content with the ease of a passing
day, and deprive not thyself of everlasting
rest. Barter not the garden of eternal
delight for the dust-heap of a mortal world.
Up from thy prison ascend unto the
glorious meads above, and from thy
mortal cage wing thy flight
unto the paradise of the Placeless.

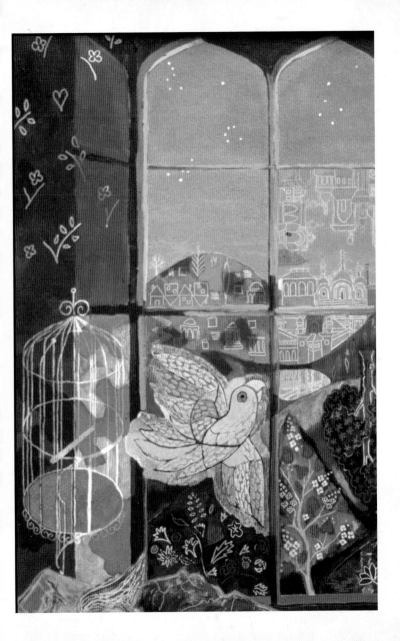

40
O MY SERVANT!

Free thyself from the fetters of this world,
and loose thy Soul from the prison of self.
Seize thy chance, for it will come
to thee no more.

41
O SON OF MY HANDMAID!

Didst thou behold immortal sovereignty,
thou wouldst strive to pass from this fleeting
world. But to conceal the one from thee and
to reveal the other is a mystery which none
but the pure in heart can comprehend.

42
O MY SERVANT!

Purge thy heart from malice and, innocent of envy, enter the divine court of holiness.

43
O MY FRIENDS!

Walk ye in the ways of the good pleasure of the Friend, and know that His pleasure is in the pleasure of His creatures. That is: no man should enter the house of his friend save at his friend's pleasure, nor lay hands upon his treasures nor prefer his own will to his friend's, and in no wise seek an advantage over him. Ponder this, ye that have insight!

44

O COMPANION OF MY THRONE!

Hear no evil, and see no evil, abase not thyself, neither sigh nor weep. Speak no evil, that thou mayest not hear it spoken unto thee, and magnify not the faults of others that thine own faults may not appear great; and wish not the abasement of anyone, that thine own abasement be not exposed. Live then the days of thy life, that are less than a fleeting moment, with thy mind stainless, thy heart unsullied, thy thoughts pure, and thy nature sanctified, so that, free and content, thou mayest put away this mortal frame, and repair unto the mystic paradise and abide in the eternal kingdom for evermore.

45

ALAS! ALAS! O LOVERS OF WORLDLY DESIRE!

Even as the swiftness of lightning ye have
passed by the Beloved One, and have set your
hearts on satanic fancies. Ye bow the knee
before your vain imaginings, and call it truth.
Ye turn your eyes towards the thorn, and
name it a flower. Not a pure breath have ye
breathed, nor hath the breeze of detachment
been wafted from the meadows of your hearts.
Ye have cast to the winds the loving counsels
of the Beloved and have effaced them
utterly from the tablet of your hearts,
and even as the beasts of the field,
ye move and have your being within
the pastures of desire and passion.

46
O BRETHREN IN THE PATH!

Wherefore have ye neglected the mention of the loved one, and kept remote from His holy presence? The essence of beauty is within the peerless pavilion, set upon the throne of glory, whilst ye busy yourselves with idle contentions. The sweet savours of holiness are breathing and the breath of bounty is wafted, yet ye are all sorely afflicted and deprived thereof. Alas for you and for them that walk in your ways and follow in your footsteps!

47
O CHILDREN OF DESIRE!

Put away the garment of vainglory, and divest yourselves of the attire of haughtiness.

In the third of the most holy lines writ and recorded in the Ruby Tablet by the pen of the unseen this is revealed:

48
O BRETHREN!

Be forbearing one with another and set not your affection on things below. Pride not yourselves in your glory, and be not ashamed of abasement. By My beauty! I have created all things from dust, and to dust will I return them again.

49
O CHILDREN OF DUST!

Tell the rich of the midnight sighing of the poor, lest heedlessness lead them into the path of destruction, and deprive them of the Tree of Wealth. To give and to be generous are attributes of Mine; well is it with him that adorneth himself with My virtues.

50
O QUINTESSENCE OF PASSION!

Put away all covetousness and seek
contentment; for the covetous hath ever
been deprived, and the contented hath
ever been loved and praised.

51
O SON OF MY HANDMAID!

Be not troubled in poverty nor confident
in riches, for poverty is followed by riches,
and riches are followed by poverty.
Yet to be poor in all save God is a wondrous
gift, belittle not the value thereof, for in the
end it will make thee rich in God, and thus
thou shalt know the meaning of the utterance,
"In truth ye are the poor," and the holy words,
"God is the all-possessing," shall even as the
true morn break forth gloriously resplendent
upon the horizon of the lover's heart, and
abide secure on the throne of wealth.

52
O CHILDREN OF NEGLIGENCE AND PASSION!

Ye have suffered My enemy to enter My house and have cast out My friend, for ye have enshrined the love of another than Me in your hearts. Give ear to the sayings of the Friend and turn towards His paradise. Worldly friends, seeking their own good, appear to love one the other, whereas the true Friend hath loved and doth love you for your own sakes; indeed He hath suffered for your guidance countless afflictions. Be not disloyal to such a Friend, nay rather hasten unto Him. Such is the day-star of the word of truth and faithfulness, that hath dawned above the horizon of the pen of the Lord of all names. Open your ears that ye may hearken unto the word of God, the Help in peril, the Self-existent.

53

O YE THAT PRIDE YOURSELVES ON MORTAL RICHES!

Know ye in truth that wealth is a mighty barrier between the seeker and his desire, the lover and his beloved. The rich, but for a few, shall in no wise attain the court of His presence nor enter the city of content and resignation. Well is it then with him, who, being rich, is not hindered by his riches from the eternal kingdom, nor deprived by them of imperishable dominion. By the Most Great Name! The splendour of such a wealthy man shall illuminate the dwellers of heaven, even as the sun enlightens the people of the earth!

54
O YE RICH ONES ON EARTH!

The poor in your midst are My trust;
guard ye My trust, and be not intent
only on your own ease.

55
O SON OF PASSION!

Cleanse thyself from the defilement of
riches and in perfect peace advance into
the realm of poverty; that from the
well-spring of detachment thou mayest
quaff the wine of immortal life.

56
O MY SON!

The company of the ungodly increaseth sorrow, whilst fellowship with the righteous cleaneth the rust from off the heart. He that seeketh to commune with God, let him betake himself to the companionship of His loved ones; and he that desireth to hearken unto the word of God, let him give ear to the words of His chosen ones.

57
O SON OF DUST!

Beware! Walk not with the ungodly and seek not fellowship with him, for such companionship turneth the radiance of the heart into infernal fire.

58
O SON OF MY HANDMAID!

Wouldst thou seek the grace of the holy
spirit, enter into fellowship with the
righteous, for he hath drunk the cup of
eternal life at the hands of the immortal
Cup-bearer and even as the true morn
doth quicken and illumine the
hearts of the dead.

59
O HEEDLESS ONES!

Think not the secrets of hearts are
hidden, nay, know ye of a certainty that in
clear characters they are engraved and
openly manifest in the holy Presence.

60
O FRIENDS!

Verily I say, whatsoever ye have
concealed within your hearts is to Us
open and manifest as the day;
but that it is hidden is of Our grace and
favour, and not of your deserving.

61
O SON OF MAN!

A dewdrop out of the fathomless ocean
of My mercy I have shed upon the peoples
of the world, yet found none turn thereunto,
inasmuch as everyone hath turned
away from the celestial wine of unity
unto the foul dregs of impurity, and,
content with mortal cup, hath put
away the chalice of immortal beauty.
Vile is that wherewith he is contented.

62
O SON OF DUST!

Turn not away thine eyes from the
matchless wine of the immortal Beloved,
and open them not to foul and mortal dregs.
Take from the hands of the divine Cup-bearer
the chalice of immortal life, that all wisdom
may be thine, and that thou mayest hearken
unto the mystic voice calling from the realm of
the invisible. Cry aloud, ye that are of low aim!
Wherefore have ye turned away from My holy
and immortal wine unto evanescent water?

63
O YE PEOPLES OF THE WORLD!

Know verily that an unforeseen
calamity is following you and that
grievous retribution awaiteth you. Think not
the deeds ye have committed have been
blotted from My sight. By My beauty!
All your doings hath My pen graven with
open characters upon tablets of chrysolite.

64

O OPPRESSORS OF EARTH!

Withdraw your hands from tyranny, for I have pledged Myself not to forgive any man's injustice. This is My covenant which I have irrevocably decreed in the preserved tablet and sealed it with My seal of glory.

65
O REBELLIOUS ONES!

My forbearance hath emboldened you
and My long-suffering hath made you
negligent, in such wise that ye have
spurred on the fiery charger of passion
into perilous ways that lead unto
destruction. Have ye thought Me
heedless or that I was unaware?

66
O EMIGRANTS!

The tongue I have designed for the
mention of Me, defile it not with
detraction. If the fire of self overcome you,
remember your own faults and not the
faults of My creatures, inasmuch as
everyone of you knoweth his own self
better than he knoweth others.

67
O CHILDREN OF FANCY!

Know verily, that while the radiant dawn
breaketh above the horizon of eternal
holiness, the satanic secrets and deeds
done in the gloom of night shall be
laid bare and manifest before the
peoples of the world.

68
O WEED THAT SPRINGETH OUT OF DUST!

Wherefore have not these soiled hands
of thine touched first thine own
garment, and why with thine heart
defiled with desire and passion dost
thou seek to commune with Me
and to enter My sacred realm?
Far, far are ye from that which ye desire.

O CHILDREN OF ADAM!

———

Holy words and pure and goodly deeds ascend
unto the heaven of celestial glory. Strive that
your deeds may be cleansed from the dust of
self and hypocrisy and find favour at the court
of glory; for ere long the assayers of mankind
shall, in the holy presence of the Adored one,
accept naught but absolute virtue and deeds
of stainless purity. This is the day-star of
wisdom and of divine mystery that hath
shone above the horizon of the divine will.
Blessed are they that turn thereunto.

O SON OF WORLDLINESS!

———

Pleasant is the realm of being, wert thou to
attain thereto; glorious is the domain of
eternity, shouldst thou pass beyond the world
of mortality; sweet is the holy ecstasy if thou
drinkest of the mystic chalice from the hands
of the celestial Youth. Shouldst thou attain this
station, thou wouldst be freed from destruction
and death, from toil and sin.

71
O MY FRIENDS!

Call ye to mind that covenant ye have entered
into with Me upon Mount Paran, situate
within the hallowed precincts of Zaman.
I have taken to witness the concourse on high
and the dwellers in the city of eternity, yet
now none do I find faithful unto the covenant.
Of a certainty pride and rebellion have
effaced it from the hearts, in such wise
that no trace thereof remaineth. Yet
knowing this, I waited and disclosed it not.

72
O MY SERVANT!

Thou art even as a finely tempered sword
concealed in the darkness of its sheath and its
value hidden from the artificer's knowledge.
Wherefore come forth from the sheath of self
and desire that thy worth may be made
resplendent and manifest unto all the world.

73
O MY FRIEND!

Thou art the day-star of the heavens of My holiness, let not the defilement of the world eclipse thy splendour. Rend asunder the veil of heedlessness, that from behind the clouds thou mayest emerge resplendent and array all things with the apparel of life.

74
O CHILDREN OF VAINGLORY!

For a fleeting sovereignty ye have abandoned My imperishable dominion, and have adorned yourselves with the gay livery of the world and made of it your boast. By My beauty! All will I gather beneath the one-coloured covering of the dust and efface all these diverse colours save them that choose My own, and that is purging from every colour.

75
O CHILDREN OF NEGLIGENCE!

Set not your affections on mortal sovereignty and rejoice not therein. Ye are even as the unwary bird that with full confidence warbleth upon the bough; till of a sudden the fowler Death throws it upon the dust, and the melody, the form and the colour are gone, leaving not a trace. Wherefore take heed, O bondslaves of desire!

76
O SON OF MY HANDMAID!

Guidance hath ever been given by words, and now it is given by deeds. Every one must show forth deeds that are pure and holy, for words are the property of all alike, whereas such deeds as these belong only to Our loved ones. Strive then with heart and soul to distinguish yourselves by your deeds. In this wise We counsel you in this holy and resplendent tablet.

O SON OF JUSTICE!

In the night-season the beauty of the immortal Being hath repaired from the emerald height of fidelity unto the Sadratu'l-Muntahá, and wept with such a weeping that the concourse on high and the dwellers of the realms above wailed at His lamenting. Whereupon there was asked, Why the wailing and weeping? He made reply: As bidden I waited expectant upon the hill of faithfulness, yet inhaled not from them that dwell on earth the fragrance of fidelity. Then summoned to return I beheld, and lo! certain doves of holiness were sore tried within the claws of the dogs of the earth. Thereupon the Maid of heaven hastened forth unveiled and resplendent from Her mystic mansion, and asked of their names, and all were told but one. And when urged, the first letter thereof was uttered, whereupon the dwellers of the celestial chambers rushed forth out of their habitation of glory. And whilst the second letter was pronounced they fell down, one and all, upon the dust. At that moment a voice was heard from the inmost shrine: "Thus far and no farther." Verily we bear witness to that which they have done and are now doing.

78
O SON OF MY HANDMAID!

Quaff from the tongue of the merciful the stream of divine mystery, and behold from the dayspring of divine utterance the unveiled splendour of the day-star of wisdom. Sow the seeds of My divine wisdom in the pure soil of the heart, and water them with the waters of certitude, that the hyacinths of knowledge and wisdom may spring up fresh and green from the holy city of the heart.

79
O SON OF DESIRE!

How long wilt thou soar in the realms of desire? Wings have I bestowed upon thee, that thou mayest fly to the realms of mystic holiness and not the regions of satanic fancy. The comb, too, have I given thee that thou mayest dress My raven locks, and not lacerate My throat.

80
O MY SERVANTS!

Ye are the trees of My garden; ye must give
forth goodly and wondrous fruits, that ye
yourselves and others may profit therefrom.
Thus it is incumbent on every one to engage in
crafts and professions, for therein lies the secret
of wealth, O men of understanding! For results
depend upon means, and the grace of God shall
be all-sufficient unto you. Trees that yield no
fruit have been and will ever be for the fire.

81
O MY SERVANT!

The basest of men are they that yield no fruit on
earth. Such men are verily counted as among
the dead, nay better are the dead in the sight of
God than those idle and worthless souls.

82
O MY SERVANT!

The best of men are they that earn a livelihood
by their calling and spend upon themselves and
upon their kindred for the love of God,
the Lord of all worlds.

The mystic and wondrous Bride,
hidden ere this beneath the veiling of
utterance, hath now, by the grace of
God and His divine favour, been made
manifest even as the resplendent light
shed by the beauty of the Beloved.
I bear witness, O friends! that the
favour is complete, the argument